Sew & Go
Kids

Jasmine Hubble

Published by
Krause Publications

700 E. State St.
Iola, WI 54045
715-445-2214
www.krause.com

Please call or write for our free catalog of publications. Our toll-free number to place an order or
obtain a free catalog is 800-258-0929 or please
use our regular business telephone 715-445-
2214 for editorial comment and further informa-
tion.

Library of Congress Catalog Number 99-65131
ISBN 0-87341-818-2

ACKNOWLEDGMENTS

THANK YOU TO PHOTOGRAPHER
KRIS KANDLER AND THE
WONDERFUL MODELS
WHO GRACE THE PAGES
OF THIS BOOK:

AMANDA AANSTAD
INDY FRITZ
CHARLEY KENNEDY
CHARLIE KOCH
BRITTANY MAZEMKE
MEGAN MAZEMKE
RYLIE SIMPSON
GRACE WHITE
MAC WHITE

INTRODUCTION

As my kids get older, I've noticed how important comfortable clothing is to them. They are busy-bodies, and fancy clothes just don't fit in with their agendas. I can't say I blame them.

This is a sequel to my book SEW & GO BABY. The idea behind this book is to offer you lots of practical, comfortable kids clothes, ranging in sizes 2 to 8 years. The patterns are simple because I know your time is limited, yet the clothing is fashionable with as few pattern pieces as possible. This allows you to decide on how much time you wish to spend on embellishing or doing appliqué.

Whether you are a new or experienced sewer, you will enjoy working with these basic patterns over and over again.

Happy Sewing!

Jasmine Hubble

ABOUT PATTERNS

The book comes complete with full-size patterns. You will find the following basic pattern pieces printed on the pattern tissue:
Basic Jacket
Basic Pants
Basic Shirt
Basic Sweatshirt

You will also find these patterns on the pattern tissue:
Appliqué Heart
Backpack Flap
Bib
Circle Template
Cow Helmet
Dinosaur Helmet
Fleece Hat
Pant Robe
Pop-up Theater
Short Blouse
Tent
Tie

All of the garments in this book are made from these patterns. The following chart will help you determine the finished garment sizes, but for the best fit I recommend:

1. For in-between sizes, trace the pattern pieces between sizes.
2. On a piece of tracing paper, trace the child you wish to sew for like a gingerbread boy or girl silhouette. Superimpose the pattern over your silhouette and easily determine the perfect fit!

FINISHED GARMENT MEASUREMENTS

Size	2 S	4 M	6 L	8 XL
Basic Jacket				
Length	14"	16"	18"	20"
Chest	28"	30"	32"	34"
Sleeve	10½"	12½"	14½"	16½"
Raincoat/Robe length	22"	24"	26"	28"
Basic Pants				
Waist (adjustable)	21"	23"	25"	26"
Inseam	12½"	15½"	19"	22½"
Hips	29"	31"	33"	35"
Length	19"	22"	25"	28"
Shorts length	12"	13"	14"	15"
Basic Shirt				
Sleeve	12"	12"	14"	16"
Chest	25"	25"	27"	28"
Length	14½"	14½"	16"	17½"
Basic Sweatshirt				
Sleeve	10½"	13"	15½"	18"
Chest	22"	24"	25"	26"
Length	14"	14½"	15"	15½"

NOTE ON SNAPS: DEPENDING ON IF THE GARMENT YOU ARE MAKING IS FOR A BOY OR GIRL, IT WILL CLOSE DIFFERENTLY: GIRLS CLOSE RIGHT TO LEFT, AND BOYS LEFT TO RIGHT.

If you use the metric system, here is a quick conversion chart:

Inches	=	Millimeters, Centimeters, Meters
0.039		1mm
0.39		1cm
39.37		1m
So,		
1/8"		3mm
1/4"		6mm
1/2"		12mm
1"		2.5cm
etc.		

Illustration Key:

Right side   Wrong side

CHAPTER 1

BED, BATH, AND SWIM FUN

This chapter is full of great basics your kids will love! The mix-and-match pajamas are sure to be a hit, the pant robe is perfect for cuddling up with a good book after bath-time, and who can resist the colorful, versatile robe and cover-up? Your kids will never leave their beach towels behind with the towel tote, and they'll flip for the fabric-covered thongs.

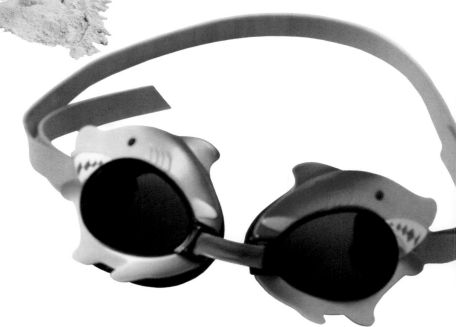

9

PAJAMAS BASICS

These are the most comfy jammies ever! You can mix and match the components— long sleeve, short sleeve, long leg, short leg, or night shirt—any way you like. The cuffs on the arms, legs, and waistband add to the comfort. Use the Ribbing Cutting Chart below to help you design your own versions. Color blocking is a great way to use up leftovers and create some great looking combinations, as shown on the short sleeve top and boxer shorts. Try making these basics in cotton, flannel, or knits.

RIBBING CUTTING CHART

All cuffs and waistbands are 6" wide. Cut neck ribbing 2½" wide. In general, the ribbing length is three-quarters the length of the opening.

Size	2	4	6	8
Arm cuffs	7"	7¼"	7½"	8"
Leg cuff	8"	8½"	9"	9½"
Waistband	23"	24"	25"	26"
Neckband	31"	31½"	32"	32½"

Note: These figures may need to be adjusted if you are working with heavy fabrics.

INSTALLING RIBBING

Here are some general directions for installing ribbing:

1. With right sides together, sew the short sides of the cuffs, forming circles. Fold the cuffs in half with wrong sides together. Make quarter markers on the cuffs and garment openings.

2. Match the cuff seams to the inside garment seams and sew in place, stretching and matching quarter markers.

LONG-SLEEVE TOP

Pattern Preparation: Use the Basic Sweatshirt pattern, following the necklines for pajamas.

DESIGNER SUGGESTION: IF YOU WANT TO ADD LACE, LIKE THAT SHOWN IN THE PHOTO, ADD IT BEFORE YOU SEW THE PIECES TOGETHER.

Cutting: Cut 1 front on fold. Cut 1 back on fold. Cut 2 sleeves. Cut ribbing, using the Ribbing Cutting Chart (page 11).

Materials and Notions

45" wide fabric:
Sizes 2 or 4: 1 yard
Sizes 6 or 8: 1¼ yards
1/2 yard of ribbing

All seam allowances are 1/4" unless otherwise stated.

1. With right sides together, sew the front to the back at the shoulders.

2. With right sides together, sew the sleeves in place to the arm openings.

3. With right sides together, sew the underarm and side seams.

4. With right sides together, sew the short sides of the arm cuffs, waistband, and neckband, forming circles. Fold each in half lengthwise, right sides out. Match one cuff seam to one arm seam and, with raw edges even and right sides together, sew in place while stretching ribbing evenly. Repeat for other arm, waistband, and neck.

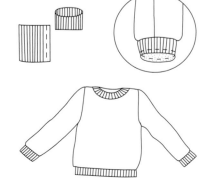

LONG PANTS

Pattern Preparation: Use the Basic Pants pattern, following the sweatpants lines on the front section. Do not trace the built-in pocket. Optional: Cut 2" off the length of the pants to add a ribbed cuff (see Ribbing Cutting Chart, page 11).

Cutting: Cut 2 fronts. Cut 2 backs.

Materials and Notions

1½ yards of 45" wide fabric or
1 yard of 60" wide fabric
1" elastic to fit waist
Optional: 6" of ribbing

All seam allowances are 1/4" unless otherwise stated.

1. With right sides together, sew the fronts to the backs at the inner and outer leg seams.

2. Turn one leg right side out and place it inside the leg that is wrong side out. Match the seams and sew the crotch in place by sewing in a horseshoe fashion. Turn pants right side out.

3. Press the top edge under 1/4". Then form a casing for the elastic by turning the top edge toward the inside 1½". Sew the casing in place, leaving an opening at center back. Insert the elastic and close opening. Optional: Topstitch across the top of the casing.

4. If not using ribbing, finish the raw edges and hem the pants by turning them up 1/2".

5. Optional: If using ribbing, with right sides together, sew the short side of the leg cuffs closed, forming circles. Fold in half lengthwise, right side out. Place one cuff over one leg opening, with raw edges even and seams matching, matching the inside leg seam. Sew in place. Repeat for other cuff.

SHORT-SLEEVE TOP

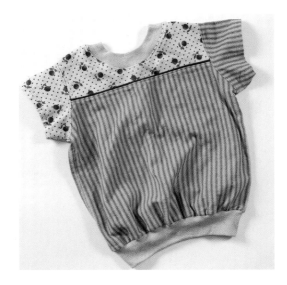

Pattern Preparation: Use the Basic Sweatshirt pattern, following the neck-line for pajamas. Follow the short sleeve lines.

DESIGNER SUGGESTION: CUT THE FRONT APART AND COLOR BLOCK BY ALTERNATING EACH HALF. WHEN YOU CUT THE PATTERN, DON'T FORGET TO ADD A 1/4" SEAM ALLOWANCE TO THE NEW CUT SIDE. PIPING, LIKE THAT SHOWN HERE, CAN ADD A NICE TOUCH.

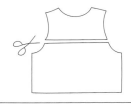

Cutting: Cut 1 front on fold. Cut 1 back on fold. Cut 2 short sleeves. Cut ribbing, using the Ribbing Cutting Chart (page 11).

Materials and Notions

3/4 yard of 45" wide fabric
6" of ribbing

All seam allowances are 1/4" unless otherwise stated.

1. With right sides together, sew the front to the back at the shoulders.

2. With right sides together, sew sleeves in place to the arm openings.

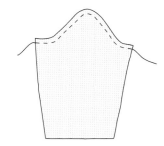

3. With right sides together, sew the underarm and side seams.

4. With right sides together, sew the short side of the waistband and neckband, forming circles. Fold the bands in half lengthwise, right sides out. Match the band seams to shirt seams and, with raw edges even and right sides together, sew in place while stretching ribbing.

5. Finish the raw edges and hem the sleeves by turning them up 1/2".

BOXER SHORTS

Pattern Preparation: Use the Basic Pants pattern, following the Shorts lines.

DESIGNER SUGGESTION: TRY CUTTING ONE HALF OF THE SHORTS ONE COLOR, AND THE OTHER HALF ANOTHER COLOR.

Cutting: Cut 2 fronts. Cut 2 backs.

Materials and Notions

1 yard of 45" wide fabric or
1/2 yard of 60" wide fabric
1" elastic, length to fit waist

Sew the shorts the same as Steps 1-4 for the Long Pants (page 13). Finish the raw edges and hem the legs by turning them up 1/2".

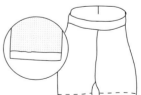

NIGHT SHIRT

Pattern Preparation: Use the Basic Sweatshirt pattern, following the neckline for pajamas. Add to the length as indicated on the pattern.

Cutting: Cut 1 front on fold. Cut 1 back on fold. Cut 2 sleeves, long or short.

Materials and Notions

For long-sleeve night shirt (shown): 1⅛ yard of 45" wide fabric
For short-sleeve night shirt: 1 yard of 45" wide fabric
6" of ribbing for cuffs (long-sleeve version)

All seam allowances are 1/4" unless otherwise stated.

1. With right sides together, sew the front to the back at the shoulders.

2. With right sides together, sew sleeves in place to the arm openings.

3. With right sides together, sew the underarm and side seams.

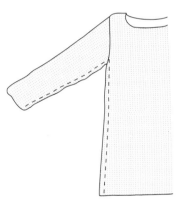

4. If making the long-sleeve version, with right sides together, sew the short sides of the cuffs, forming circles. Fold each in half lengthwise, right sides out. Match one cuff seam to one arm seam and, with raw edges even and right sides together, sew in place while stretching ribbing. Repeat for other arm. Repeat for neckband (either version). For short sleeves, finish the raw edges and hem the sleeves by turning them up 1/2".

PANT ROBE WITH HOOD

In our house, we nick-named this the "wonder-suit." You can make it out of anything—our sample was made from Berber—and use it for anything, including a snowsuit, rainsuit, or terry robe. It's comfortable and a winner with every kid!

THE ELEVENTH HOUR   Graeme Base   Abrams

PRECIOUS MOMENTS   Bedtime Stories

Pattern Preparation: Use the Pant Robe pattern.

Cutting: Cut 2 fronts. Cut 2 backs. Cut 2 sleeves. Optional: cut 2 hoods and cut 2 hood linings.

Materials and Notions

Suggested fabrics: terry, fleece, berber, knits, nylon, polarfleece

Size	2	4	6	8
45"	1¼ yds	1⅜ yds	2⅝ yds	3 yds
60"	1¼ yds	1⅜ yds	1⅝ yds	1¾yds
Zipper	14"	16"	18"	20"

2 large grommets
1¼ yards drawstring
12" of ribbing (20" or 24" wide)
Optional: If using neck ribbing instead of hood, cut 3" wide. This finished width will be 1¼" (the length is three-quarters of the opening).

Ribbing for Arm and Leg Cuffs
Cut all cuffs 6" wide

Size	2	4	6	8
Legs	8"	9"	9½"	10"
Arms	7"	7½"	8"	8½"

Note: Depending on how heavy your fabric is and how much your ribbing stretches, you may need to adjust the cuff lengths a little. As a rule of thumb, the cuff length is three-quarters of what the opening is.

All seam allowances are 1/4" unless otherwise stated. Mark the center front line for zipper placement.

1. With right sides together, sew the center backs together.

2. With right sides together, sew the fronts to the back at the shoulders.

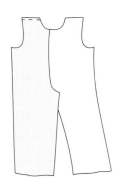

3. With right sides together, sew the sleeves in place to the arm openings.

4. With right sides together, close the underarm and side seams.

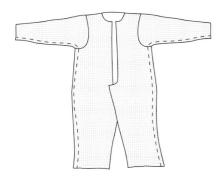

5. With right sides together, close the center front to the notched zipper opening. Clip to dot.

6. With right sides together, sew the inside leg seams.

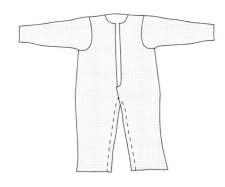

7. With right sides together, sew the short sides of the leg and arm cuffs, forming circles. Fold the cuffs in half with wrong sides together. Make quarter markers on the cuffs, arms, and legs.

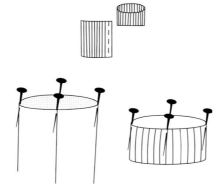

8. Match the leg cuff seams to the inside leg seams and sew in place, stretching and matching quarter markers. Repeat for arms.

9. Optional: Repeat Steps 7 and 8 for neck ribbing. Use a 3" wide piece of ribbing three-quarters the length of the neck opening.

10. If making the hooded version, with right sides together, sew hood pieces together. Repeat for lining.

11. Place the two hoods (fabric and lining) right sides together and sew around the front opening. Turn, press, and edgestitch around the hood opening from the right side. Set grommets for the drawstring on each hood side, up far enough so you can still sew the hood to the robe and close to the edgestitching.

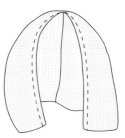

12. Match the center back of the hood to the center back of the neck with right sides together. Sew the hood in place, but not the lining. Press the raw edge of the hood lining under and stitch in the ditch to the hood. Stitch a second time around the hood front opening, approximately 1/2" from the front edge to form a casing for the drawstring.

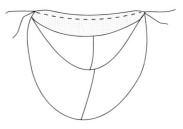

13. Insert the drawstring. Baste the zipper and sew in place. Cut the zipper to fit the bottom, if necessary.

BATH OR SWIM ROBE

BRIGHT AND CHEERFUL, THIS ROBE FEATURES A SOFT STRETCH TERRY THAT MAKES THE INSIDE WARM AND COZY, SO IT IS GREAT FOR WEARING AT HOME, THE BEACH, OR FOR SWIMMING LESSONS. DON'T FORGET TO MAKE THE MATCHING TOWEL TOTE! NOT JUST FOR KIDS, THE TOTE MAKES A GREAT GIFT IDEA FOR ANYONE TO TAKE TO SWIMMING OR TO THE GYM—YOU'LL NEVER LOSE THE TOWEL BECAUSE IT'S PART OF THE BAG.

Pattern Preparation: Use the Basic Jacket pattern, following the Raincoat/Robe lines. If you are using this as a basic robe, you probably won't line it. Clean finish the raw edges and use 1/2" hems.

Cutting: Cut 2 fronts, 2 hoods, and 2 sleeves of fabric and stretch terry. Cut 1 back on fold fabric and 1 back on fold stretch terry. Cut 2 cord tab ends 1½" x 3" out of fabric (no pattern piece). Cut 1 belt 4½" x 44" (no pattern piece).

Materials and Notions

2 yards of 45" wide fabric
1⅓ yards of 60" wide stretch terry
5 snaps, size 24 or 32

All seam allowances are 1/4" unless otherwise stated.

The following directions refer to the fabric side. Repeat Step 1-5 with the terry side.

1. With right sides together, sew the fronts to the back at the shoulders.

2. With right sides together, sew the sleeves in place to the arm openings.

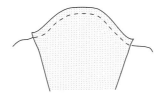

3. With right sides together, close the underarm and side seams.

4. With right sides together, sew the hoods together.

5. Matching center backs, with right sides together, sew the hood to the robe and hood lining to the robe lining.

6. Matching corners and seams, place the two robes right sides together. Sew from center bottom around the front, around the hood, and down the other side. Leave a generous opening at center back bottom to work on the sleeves.

7. Turn the robe right side out (fabric side out). Turn the sleeve's raw edges toward the wrong side, matching seams. Stick a pin into the folded raw edge on each side so when you turn the sleeve inside out, you can find this spot again. Remove it later.

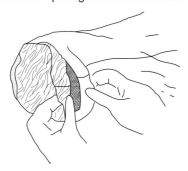

8. Reach up into the robe from the center bottom opening and grab the sleeve where it is pinned. Bag the sleeve by placing the fabric and terry sleeves right sides together and sewing around the sleeve's raw edge only. Turn right side out. From the right side, topstitch around the sleeve opening. Repeat for other sleeve.

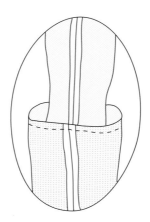

9. Edgestitch around the hoods. Mark the location for a grommet to pull the drawstring through; set one on each side by going through the bottom opening. Stitch around the hood again, forming a 1/2" casing. Insert the drawstring.

10. Topstitch around the entire jacket, closing the opening at the bottom.

11. Evenly space the snaps down the front of the robe. With right sides together, sew the belt lengthwise, turn, and press with the seam running down the center. Turn ends in and stitch belt closed. Stitch belt to the robe's center back, at the wearer's waistline.

12. With right sides together, sew the side and across the bottom of the cord tabs. Turn and stick the end of the drawstring in the tab, pushing the raw edges of fabric inward. Sew back and forth across the top, securing the cord in place.

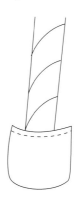

TOWEL TOTE

This whole idea got started when my kids took swimming lessons. The towels would get left behind and it seemed like we were carrying so much stuff. This tote is the perfect answer to the problem and it makes a great gift for any age. Pair it up with a matching set of thongs that take only minutes to do.

Pattern Preparation: Note that there are no patterns for this project.

Cutting: Cut 2 bag pieces 35" x 18½". Cut 1 band piece 35" x 6" with interfacing. Cut 1 cord tab 4" x 4½".

Materials and Notions

1 bath sheet or beach towel
1¼ yards of 45" wide fabric
2 yards drawstring
8 large grommets
35" x 6" piece of interfacing

All seam allowances are 1/4" unless otherwise stated.

1. Fold each bag piece with right sides together and sew down the side and across the bottom.

2. To give the bag some depth, pull the bottom seam of the bag apart and stitch across the triangle tip 1½". Place bags wrong sides together and set aside.

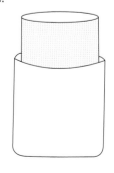

3. With right sides together, sew the short ends of the band closed and press. Press in half lengthwise, right side out. Match the band seam with the bag seam and sew in place. If you have a serger, it is good to clean finish the band's raw edge; if not, use a fancy stitch to sew the band flat to the bag so it will look nice from both sides.

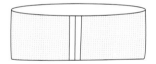

4. Evenly space and set the grommets, four on each bag half.

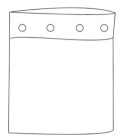

5. Position the bag on the upper left corner of the towel, allowing the band portion of the bag to extend beyond the upper edge of the towel, and the seam of the bag matching the left edge of the towel.

6. Sew the bag to the towel on the left side, 1/2" in from the left edge.

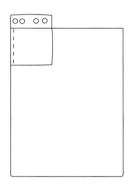

7. Sew the bag to the towel on the right side, 1/2" in toward the bag side.

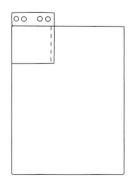

8. Fold the cord tab in half so it is 2" wide. With right sides together, sew down the side and across the bottom. Turn the top raw edge back 1/4" and press. Turn the cord tab right side out.

9. Insert the drawstring by starting at the left end, weaving it in and out and then ending on the left end again. Pull the cord so the ends are even. Tape or knot the cord ends. Insert the cord ends into the cord tab, making sure the raw edges are turned toward the inside. Stitch across the top twice, securing the cord.

10. Attach the cord tab end to the bag by stitching it right into the squared-off seam of the bag bottom on the left.

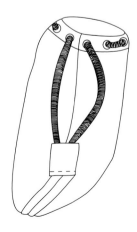

11. To get the towel back into the bag, reach into the bag, grabbing the towel and then pulling it while turning the bag inside out.

THONGS

THIS IS A QUICK, EASY, AND INEXPENSIVE PROJECT—A MUST-HAVE FOR A DAY AT THE BEACH!

Pattern Preparation: Note that there are no patterns for this project.

Cutting: Cut fabric strips 1½" wide in length required to wrap around thong.

Materials and Notions

Fabric
Hot glue gun and sticks
Optional: bias tape marker

1. Press fabric's raw edges 1/4" toward the middle. If you have a bias tape maker, it will come in handy.

2. Using a hot glue gun, glue the beginning of the fabric strip on the inside of the thong. Wrap around the sling, overlapping the fabric slightly. At the toe, go under and come up the other side. Continue wrapping in the same fashion. Cut off any excess fabric and glue the end in place.

TERRY TOWEL SWIM COVER-UP

YOU DON'T HAVE TO GO SWIMMING TO WEAR THIS EXCITING TERRY JACKET. CHOOSE YOUR FAVORITE BEACH TOWEL AND SEW AWAY! I LINED THIS SAMPLE WITH NYLON SUPLEX, SO IT IS ACTUALLY REVERSIBLE.

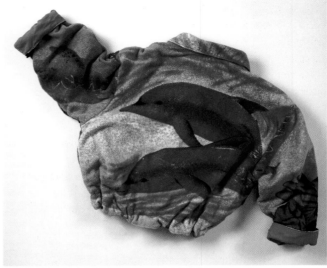

Pattern Preparation: Use the Basic Jacket pattern. On front section, follow the jacket to the placket foldline. Interface the fronts with a 1¼" strip of sturdy interfacing on both the towel and lining. Interface the lining collar only. Interface the grommet area with a 1½" square.

Cutting: Cut 2 fronts. Cut 1 back on fold. Cut 2 sleeves. Cut 1 collar. Repeat for lining. Optional hood, cut 2.

Materials and Notions

- 1 large beach towel
- 1 yard of 60" lining
- 2 grommets
- 1 yard drawstring
- 5 snaps

All seam allowances are 1/4" unless otherwise stated. Press the seams as you go.

Tip: Use a ball-point needle while sewing the terry and a sharp needle for sewing the nylon.

1. With right sides together, sew the fronts to the back at the shoulders.

2. With right sides together, sew the sleeves in place to the arm openings.

3. With right sides together, close the underarm and side seams.

4. With right sides together and the collar's center back matching the jacket's center back, sew the lining collar to the terry jacket and the terry collar to the jacket lining. If you are adding the optional hood, sew it to the jacket now (see page 22, Step 5).

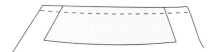

5. Take the two separate jackets and place them right sides together. Sew from the center bottom around the front, across the collar, and down the other side. Leave a generous opening at center back bottom to work on the sleeves. Clip in at the collar corner.

6. Turn the jacket right side out (towel side out). Turn the sleeves' raw edges toward the wrong side, matching seams. Stick a pin into the folded raw edge on each side so when you turn the sleeve inside out, you can find this spot again. Remove it later.

7. Reach up into the jacket from the center bottom opening and grab the sleeve where it is pinned. Bag the sleeve by placing the towel and lining sleeves together and sewing around the raw edge. Turn right side out. Topstitch around the sleeve opening. Stitch in the ditch through the collars. Repeat for other sleeve.

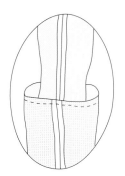

8. From the bottom opening, set the grommets for the drawstring 1" up from the jacket's bottom and 3" in from the front edge.

9. Topstitch around entire jacket, closing the bottom opening. For the drawstring, stitch across the bottom again, 2" up. For the snap placket, stitch up the front 1" in from the edge.

10. Evenly set the snaps and insert the drawstring.

2 PLAY CLOTHES

Play clothes for year 'round outdoor and indoor fun are found in this chapter. From the sporty Short-sleeve Hooded Camp Shirt and Shorts and Hooded Sweatshirt and Sweatpants, to the Long and Short Fleece Vests, Jams, and Hat, your kids will look great while biking, hiking, or playing in the yard. Overalls are the ultimate in kids' playwear, and paired with the Zip-front Hooded Shirt and Basic Reversible Jacket, it is the basis for a great outfit. Why not recycle an old pair of jeans and make the Denim Shirt/Jacket or use clear tablecloth vinyl to make a knock-out raincoat?

SHORT-SLEEVE HOODED CAMP SHIRT

BRIGHT, CHEERY FABRICS, AS SHOWN ON THE SAMPLE, MAKE THIS SHIRT A SUMMER KNOCK-OUT. THE HOOD WILL HELP PROTECT DELICATE SKIN IN THE SUN'S RAYS. PAIR IT WITH THE SHORTS FOR AN UNFORGETTABLE LOOK.

Pattern Preparation: Follow the Basic Sweatshirt pattern, cutting on the placket line and using the Sweatshirt necklines. Use short sleeves. Interface the front placket.

Cutting: Cut 2 fronts. Cut 1 back on fold. Cut 2 sleeves. Cut 4 hoods (2 lining).

Materials and Notions

3/4 yard of 45" wide fabric
5 snaps
Interfacing

All seam allowances are 1/4" unless otherwise stated.

1. With right sides together, sew the fronts to the back at the shoulders.

2. With right sides together, sew the sleeves in place to the arm openings.

3. With right sides together, close the underarm and side seams.

4. Press up the lower hem (shirt bottom and sleeves) 1/2" and stitch in place.

5. With right sides together, sew the hood and hood lining together at the center back seams. Place the two hoods right sides together and sew around the center front and down the short side.

6. Attach the hood to the shirt by matching the hood's center back to the shirt and at center front. Wrap the placket around the hood toward the inside. Stitch the hood in place. Turn the raw edge of the inside hood under and sew the hood in place.

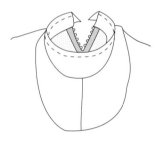

7. Turn the placket right side out and stitch in place.

8. Evenly set the snaps.

SHORTS

KIDS CAN NEVER HAVE ENOUGH PAIRS OF SHORTS. THESE CAN HAVE BUILT-IN POCKETS, WHICH TAKE ONLY SECONDS TO INSTALL (THE SAMPLE SHOWN DOESN'T HAVE POCKETS; FOLLOW THE INSTRUCTIONS ON PAGE 15).

Pattern Preparation: Use the Basic Pants pattern, following the lines for the Shorts and using the built-in pocket pattern.

Cutting: Cut 2 fronts, including the pocket. Cut 2 backs.

Materials and Notions

1¼ yards of 45" wide cotton fabric
1" wide elastic to fit waist

All seam allowances are 1/4" unless otherwise stated.

1. Press the pocket in place by folding it accordion-style, first to the back, and then to the front on the foldlines marked on the pattern. The rounded bottom edges of the pocket should be even and the sides straight. Stitch the bottom of the pocket closed.

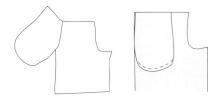

2. With right sides together, sew the fronts to the backs at the sides and inside leg seams.

3. Turn one leg right side out and place it inside the leg that is inside out.

4. Sew around the crotch in a horseshoe fashion. Turn the shorts right side out.

5. Press and stitch the top edge 1¼" toward the wrong side to form a casing. Leave an opening at center back. Insert the elastic and close the opening.

6. Hem the shorts by pressing up the lower raw edge 1/2" and stitch in place.

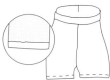

LONG FLEECE VEST

THIS IS ONE OF
THOSE VESTS
(SHOWN AT RIGHT)
KIDS WILL LIVE IN.
YOU MIGHT EVEN
HAVE TO PUT UP A
FIGHT TO GET IT IN
THE WASH! OUR
SAMPLE WAS MADE
WITH FLEECE, BUT IT
IS ALSO IDEAL FOR
BERBER OR EVEN
CORDUROY.

Pattern Preparation: Use the Basic Jacket pattern, adding 2" in length. Interface the front placket with a 1½" wide strip of sturdy interfacing.

Cutting: Cut 2 fronts. Cut 1 back on fold. Cut 2 collars on fold and cut 1 interfacing.

Materials and Notions

45" wide fabric
Sizes 2 or 4: 3/4 yard
Sizes 6 or 8: 1¼ yards

60" wide fabric
Sizes 2 or 4: 5/8 yard
Sizes 6 or 8: 3/4 yard

1/4 yard of interfacing
5 snaps, size 24
Optional: 1" wide fold-over elastic

All seam allowances are 1/4" unless otherwise stated.

1. With right sides together, sew the fronts to the back at the shoulders.

2. Turn the finished armhole edges toward the wrong side 1/4" and stitch in place. Optional: use 1" fold-over elastic binding all around the vest.

3. With right sides together, sew the side seams.

4. Clean finish the lower edge, turn it up 1/2", and stitch in place.

5. With right sides together, sew the collar pieces, leaving the bottom open. Clip the curves and corners and turn.

6. Attach the lower collar to the vest, matching center backs. Fold the placket back, extending over the upper collar, and stitch in place. Turn the collar's remaining raw edge under and stitch in place.

7. Topstitch the placket in place.

8. Evenly set the snaps.

SHORT FLEECE VEST

THIS SHORT VEST IS NOT ONLY FASHIONABLE BUT IS ALSO PRACTICAL. THANKS TO PRE-MADE FOLD-OVER BINDING, THIS BECOMES A VERY QUICK AND EASY SEWING PROJECT. IF SEWING WITH FLEECE, THERE'S NO NEED TO FINISH THE RAW EDGES. DON'T BE SURPRISED IF YOU GET REQUESTS FOR MORE!

Pattern Preparation: Use the Basic Jacket pattern, following the Short Vest lines. Interface the front placket with a 1½" wide strip of sturdy interfacing.

Cutting: Cut 2 fronts. Cut 1 back on fold.

DESIGNER SUGGESTION: HAVING TROUBLE LOCATING FOLD-OVER ELASTIC? YOU CAN MAKE YOUR OWN THAT WILL LOOK VERY PROFESSIONAL. PURCHASE 60" WIDE LYCRA (SUCH AS SWIMSUIT FABRIC) AND CUT IT INTO 3" WIDE STRIPS. FOLD IT IN HALF, RIGHT SIDES OUT, AND SEW IT TO THE WRONG SIDE USING A 1/4" SEAM. FLIP TO THE RIGHT SIDE AND TOPSTITCH IN PLACE.

Materials and Notions

1/2 yard of 60" fabric
Interfacing for snap placket
1½ yards of 1" wide fold-over elastic or other fold-over binding
1 yard of 1/4" elastic
4 snaps, size 32

All seam allowances are 1/4" unless otherwise stated.

1. With right sides together, sew the fronts to the back at the side seams.

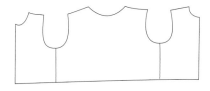

2. Place the fold-over elastic over the raw edges of the armholes and zigzag in place using a three-step zigzag stitch. Adjust the stitch width to catch both the fleece and elastic. Sew the shoulder seams closed.

3. Repeat this process around the neck opening. Pull just a little on the fold-over elastic to keep the neck from puckering.

4. Form a casing at the vest bottom by folding up the raw edge toward the wrong side 1/2". Edgestitch the casing in place. Edgestitch across bottom edge.

5. Insert the elastic and pull to gather the fabric slightly, but not too tight. Secure the elastic at the ends, or use 1" fold-over elastic; pull firmly while sewing.

6. Clean finish the placket's raw edges, fold it 3/4" back, and edgestitch in place, tucking the end of the fold-over elastic under the placket. Edgestitch again close to the fold.

7. Evenly set the snaps.

FLEECE HAT

REGARDLESS OF WHERE YOU LIVE, A HAT CAN PROTECT YOUR CHILD'S EARS DURING THE WINTER MONTHS. THIS HAT CAN BE MADE TO MATCH ANY OF YOUR CHILD'S OUTERWEAR.

Pattern Preparation: Use the Fleece Hat pattern.

Cutting: Cut 1 on fold.

Materials and Notions

1/3 yard fabric

All seam allowances are 1/4" unless otherwise stated.

1. With right sides together, sew the hat section together.

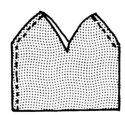

2. Sew the pairs together to form a half circle.

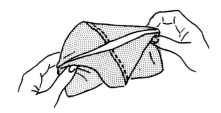

3. Clean- finish the lower hat edge and roll up.

JAMS

THESE ARE A GREAT LENGTH FOR SKATE BOARDING OR BEACH COMBING. I PAIRED THESE BERBER JAMS WITH THE LONG AND SHORT VESTS. SEW THESE THE SAME AS THE SHORTS ON PAGE 34, BUT ADD 4" TO LENGTH ON THE BASIC PANTS PATTERN.

HOODED SWEATSHIRT

You can't beat these thick, comfy, cozy sweats. The waistband, ribbing, and cuffs ensure comfort from top to bottom.

Pattern Preparation: Use the Basic Sweatshirt pattern, following the Sweatshirt neckline and the foldline on center front.

Cutting: From main color, cut 1 front and 1 back on the fold (both 2½" shorter in length than the pattern shows because you are adding a ribbed waistband). Cut 2 hoods. From contrasting fabric, cut 2 sleeves and 2 hoods. Cut one zipper facing piece 2" wide and 4½" long (no pattern piece); interface this piece. Cut 2 sleeve cuffs and 1 waistband from ribbing. The cuffs should be 4½" wide and 6½" long. The band should be 6" wide and 24" long.

Materials and Notions

1 yard of main color fabric*
3/4 yard of contrasting color fabric*
1" wide elastic to fit waist
1¼ yards drawstring
2 large grommets
1/3 yard ribbing
7" zipper with optional pull

*If using fleece, use a pressing sheet or cloth for Step 1.

All seam allowances are 1/4" unless otherwise stated. Mark the center front line for zipper placement.

1. With right sides together, place the interfaced zipper facing piece on the center front foldline and mark where the slit ends (see pattern). From the top of the neck, sew down to the slit mark and back up to the top of the neck, making the distance between the slit approximately 1/8" wide. Cut down the middle of the slit and angle into the corners. Turn and press the facing toward the wrong side.

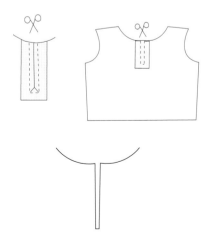

2. With right sides together, sew the front to the back at the shoulders.

3. With right sides together, sew the hoods together. With right sides together, sew the hood lining from contrasting fabric together. Place the two hoods (hood and lining) with right sides together and sew around the front edge. Do not sew down the center front of the hood.

4. Determine the location of the grommets for the drawstring. From the wrong side of the front hood, iron a scrap of interfacing to reinforce the area for the grommets. Set the grommets in place about 1" in.

5. With right sides together, sew the outside hood to the neckline, leaving the lining free.

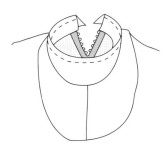

6. Baste the zipper in place, starting at the bottom of the slit, turning the hood's raw edges inward 1/4", and sandwiching the zipper between the hood and hood lining. Sew the zipper in place.

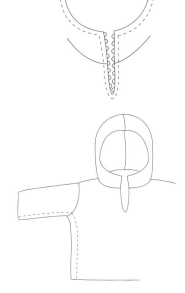

7. For the drawstring casing, first edgestitch around the hood and then again, approximately 1¼" from the edge. (The grommet should be in the middle of the casing.) Turn the raw edge of the inside hood under and sew the hood in place.

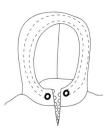

8. With right sides together, sew the sleeves in place to the arm openings.

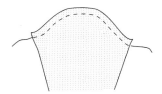

9. With right sides together, close the underarm and side seams.

10. With right sides together, sew the short sides of the cuffs and waistband closed, forming circles. Fold in half with wrong sides together so the seams are on the inside.

11. With right sides together, raw edges even, and the cuffs' and band's seams matching the sweatshirt's seams, sew ribbing in place, stretching while sewing.

SWEATPANTS

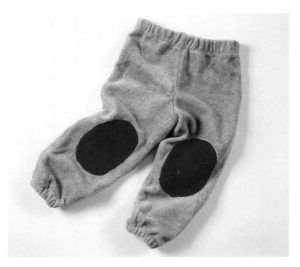

THESE ARE THE PERFECT PANTS FOR OUTSIDE SPORTS OR JUST LOUNGING AROUND HOME ON A LAZY AFTERNOON. ADD OPTIONAL KNEE PADS (SHOWN HERE) FOR EXTRA DURABILITY.

Pattern Preparation: Use the Basic Pants pattern, following the Sweatpants lines on the front section. Do not trace the pocket (although you can add your own side seam pocket).

DESIGNER SUGGESTION: THE KNEE PADS CAN BE CUT FROM CONTRASTING SCRAPS IN ANY DESIRED SHAPE. ADD TO THE FRONT SECTIONS BEFORE SEWING THE PANTS TOGETHER.

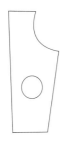

Cutting: Cut 2 fronts. Cut 2 backs.

Materials and Notions

45" wide fabric:
Size 2: 1⅓ yards
Size 4: 1½ yards
Size 6: 1¾ yards
Size 8: 2 yards
1/2 yard of 3/8" elastic

All seam allowances are 1/4" unless otherwise stated.

1. With right sides together, sew the fronts to the backs at the inner and outer leg seams.

2. Turn one leg right side out and place it inside the leg that is inside out. Match seams and sew the crotch in place by sewing in a horse-shoe fashion.

3. Finish raw edge and form a casing for the elastic by turning the top edge toward the inside 1-1/4". Sew the casing in place, leaving an opening at center back. Insert the elastic and close the opening.

4. To add elastic to the legs, form a casing by turning the raw edge up 1/2" and stitch in place, leaving an opening. Insert elastic and close the opening.

OVERALLS

OVERALLS ARE THE BEST PLAY PANTS. WHETHER THEY ARE FOR A BOY OR GIRL, ANY OF THE TOPS IN THIS BOOK WILL COMPLEMENT THEM. WE PAIRED OURS WITH THE BASIC JACKET AND KNITTED ZIP-FRONT HOODED SHIRT.

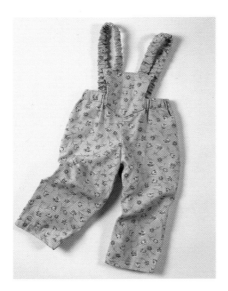

Pattern Preparation: Use the Basic Pants pattern, following the built-in pocket on the front section. You will also use the Bib pattern piece.

Cutting: Cut 2 fronts with built-in pocket. Cut 2 backs. Cut 2 bibs (interface 1). Cut 2 straps, 2¾" x 18-24" (no pattern piece).

Materials and Notions

45" wide fabric:
Size 2: 1⅓ yards
Size 4: 1½ yards
Size 6: 1¾ yards
Size 8: 2 yards
1½ yards of 1" wide elastic

All seam allowances are 1/4" unless otherwise stated.

1. Press the pocket in place by folding it accordion-style, first to the back (wrong sides together) and then to the front on the foldlines marked on the pattern. The rounded bottom edges of the pocket should be even and the sides straight. Topstitch along the foldline that has the fabric wrong sides together first and then stitch the bottom of the pocket closed.

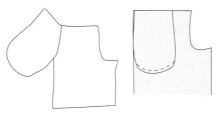

2. With right sides together, sew the fronts to the backs at the sides and inside leg seams.

3. Turn one leg right side out and place it inside the leg that is inside out. Sew around the crotch in a horseshoe fashion. Turn the pants right side out.

4. Press the top edge down 1/4" and then 1¼". Sew the casing in place, leaving an opening to insert the elastic at center front. Do not insert the elastic yet.

5. Sew the bib right sides together, leaving an opening at the top to turn and later insert the suspenders. Clip, turn, and press.

6. With right sides together, sew the straps closed. Turn and press them with the seam running down center back. Insert the elastic and secure at one end by sewing back and forth. Leave the elastic hanging out on the opposite end for now. (Your finished elastic length will be somewhere between 8" to 14". Do not cut the elastic yet.)

7. Position the bib with pins so the lower side points are even with the stitching from the casing. Insert the secured ends of the straps in the top of the bib. Insert the waist elastic, allowing it to stop and start where the bib is. Adjust the elastic to fit the waist and secure the ends while sewing the bib in place. Sew around the entire bib.

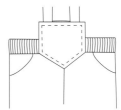

8. Finish the ends on the straps by determining the desired length. You may find it necessary to shorten the straps as well as the elastic. Turn the fabric's raw edge in 1/4" and secure the elastic ends. Stitch to the back of the overalls, following the stitching from the casing.

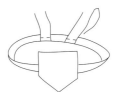

9. Hem the pants by pressing up the lower raw edge 1/2" and stitching in place or clean finish the raw edge.

ZIP-FRONT HOODED SHIRT

THIS SHIRT CAN BE MADE WITH EITHER LONG OR SHORT SLEEVES. USE FUN, COMFORTABLE FABRICS, SUCH AS WAFFLE KNITS OR PICOT FRENCH TERRY CLOTH.

Pattern Preparation: Use the Basic Sweatshirt pattern.

Cutting: Cut 1 front on fold. Cut 1 back on fold. Cut 2 sleeves, adding 2½" to the length. Cut 4 hoods. Cut a zipper facing 2" wide and 4½" long (no pattern piece); interface it.

Materials and Notions

1⅜ yards of fabric
7" zipper

All seam allowances are 1/4" unless otherwise stated. Mark the center front line for zipper placement.

1. With right sides together, place the interfaced zipper facing piece on the center front foldline and mark where the slit ends (see pattern). From the top of the neck, sew down to the slit mark and back up to the top of the neck, making the distance between the slit approximately 1/8" wide. Cut down the middle of the slit and angle into the corners. Turn and press the facing toward wrong side.

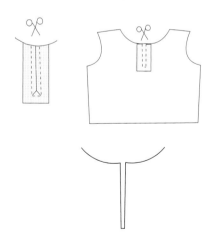

2. With right sides together, sew the front to the back at the shoulders.

3. With right sides together, sew the hoods together and the hood lining. Place the two hoods with right sides together and sew around the front edge. Do not sew down the center front of the hood.

4. With right sides together, sew the outside of the hood to the neckline.

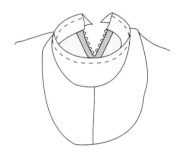

5. Baste the zipper in place, starting at the bottom of the slit, turning the hood's raw edges inward 1/4", and sandwiching the zipper between the hood and hood lining. Sew the zipper in place.

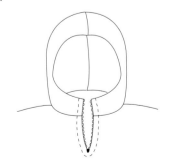

6. Turn the raw edge of the inside hood under and sew the hood in place.

7. With right sides together, sew the sleeves in place to the arm openings.

8. With right sides together, close the underarm and side seams.

9. Hem the sleeves by pressing up 1/2" and then stitching the hem in place with a twin needle or double stitching hem. Repeat for shirt hem, but press up 1".

BASIC REVERSIBLE JACKET

At the beginning of every school year I make this jacket for my kids. It's so practical and comfortable and, being reversible, it matches a variety of their garments. It's so simple to sew that now my 12-year-old makes her own!

Pattern Preparation: Use the Basic Jacket pattern, following the Jacket cutting lines. On the front section, follow the jacket to the placket foldline. Interface the fronts with a 1¼" strip of sturdy interfacing on both the jacket and lining. Interface the lining collar only. Interface the grommet area with a 1½" square.

Cutting: Cut 2 fronts. Cut 1 back on fold. Cut 2 sleeves. Cut 1 collar. Repeat for the lining. Cut 2 cuffs 2½" wide and 6½" long (no pattern piece). The hood is optional; cut 2 fabric and 2 lining.

Materials and Notions

1¼ yards of 60" fabric for each side (fabric and lining)
1½" wide elastic
10 snaps, 5 to match each side
6" of ribbing

All seam allowances are 1/4" unless otherwise stated. Press the seams as you go. Repeat Steps 1-3 for the jacket lining.

1. With right sides together, sew the fronts to the back at the shoulders.

2. With right sides together, sew the sleeves in place to the arm openings.

3. With right sides together, sew the underarm and side seams closed.

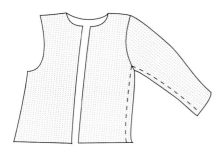

4. Reverse the colors when attaching the collars. With right sides together, sew the lining collar to the jacket side and the jacket collar to the lining side (see page 22, Step 5).

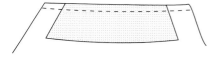

5. Take the two separate jackets and place them right sides together. Sew from the center bottom around the front, across the collar, and down the other side. Leave a generous opening at center back bottom to work on the sleeves. Leave a 2" opening at the center front opening at the very bottom so you can insert the elastic later. Clip in at the collar corner, turn, and press.

6. Turn the jacket right side out (fabric on the outside). Sew the short side of the cuffs closed, forming circles. With the raw edges even and right sides together, sew the cuffs to the sleeves, matching the cuffs' seams with the sleeves' seams.

7. Reach up into the jacket from the center bottom opening and grab the sleeves. Bag the sleeves by placing the ribbing inside of the lining sleeves. With raw edges even and right sides together, sew the other end of the ribbing to the lining side of the sleeve. Turn right side out. Stitch in the ditch through the collars.

8. Make an elastic casing by sewing the bottom opening closed, stitching 1¾" from the edge. Edgestitch along the bottom again. Insert a piece of elastic (approximately three-quarters of the bottom length) through the opening at bottom center front. Secure it 1½" in from both ends. Pull just enough to gather the jacket slightly to give it some style. Each elastic responds differently, so secure one side first and then check the other side before cutting.

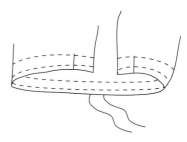

9. Edgestitch the center front and then 1½" in again to form a snap placket. Evenly set the snaps down the center front. To do a reversible snap installation, set the top snaps on the outside of the jacket first, then discard the back (last) component of the snap and replace it with another top that will match the other side of the jacket.

RAINCOAT

PERFECT FOR SPLASHING AROUND,
THIS RAINCOAT ALLOWS YOU TO
CHOOSE ANY FABRIC BECAUSE THE
OUTSIDE IS COVERED WITH HEAVY
VINYL.

Pattern Preparation: Use the Basic Jacket pattern, following the lines for the Raincoat/Robe. Add 3" to the sleeve length.

Cutting: Cut 2 fronts. Cut 1 back on fold. Cut 2 sleeves. Cut 2 collars. Interface the snap placket. After cutting out the fabric pieces, lay the pieces right sides up and put clear vinyl on top of them. Cut out the vinyl using the fabric pieces as guides. Cut 1 vinyl collar only! The hood is optional and can be used in place of the collar; cut 2 fabric, 1 vinyl.

Materials and Notions

45" wide cotton print
Sizes 2 or 4: 1¾ yards
Sizes 6 or 8: 2¼ yards
1¾ yards of clear tablecloth vinyl
5 snaps, size 24
2" wide strip of interfacing

All seam allowances are 1/4" unless otherwise stated. Clean finish the raw edges of the fabric pieces only.

Note: Sewing instructions apply to one vinyl piece on top of one fabric piece.

1. With right sides together, sew the fronts to the back at the shoulders.

2. With right sides together, sew the sleeves in place to the arm openings.

3. With right sides together, sew the sleeves, underarm, and side seams closed.

4. Turn up a 1" hem on the sleeves and topstitch in place.

5. With right sides together, sew the collar together with the vinyl in the middle. Clip corners and turn (if adding the hood, see page 21, Steps 4 and 5).

6. Pin the lower collar to the neck, matching center backs. Fold the placket back right sides together and sew to upper collar. Turn placket.

7. Turn the collar's raw edge under and edgestitch in place.

8. Topstitch the placket and edgestitch close to the fold.

9. Evenly set the snaps.

DENIM SHIRT/JACKET

Here is a great idea for recycling those out-of-style tight-legged jeans, the ones with the holes in the knees that don't fit anymore. Depending on the size shirt you are making, you need two to three old pairs of jeans.

This is a project you can really have fun with, so get creative and don't worry about doing anything wrong, because you weren't going to use the jeans again to begin with! Reuse the pockets, belt loops, brand name patches, etc. to give your creation that real denim look. For the sample, I cut the sleeves using a very tight pair of legs that had ankle zippers. I skipped making cuffs and just cut the sleeves longer to compensate for the cuff length.

Use the Basic Shirt pattern. Cut the jeans open along the inside leg seams for maximum yardage. On the front, make sure you have a right and left front in the end. Plan on using the double-seams decoratively as you cut the pattern pieces. For the final touch, I added buttons from real jeans (which can be set with just a household hammer) and a baseball jacket-style collar.

Once your shirt pieces are cut out, add any goodies such as pockets and patches. Sew the shirt just like the Country Shirt on page 68, omitting the pleats. Fold the rib collar in half lengthwise and sew to the neck in place of the conventional collar.

DESIGNER SUGGESTION: TO MAKE SEWING OVER THICK SEAMS A BREEZE, TRY USING A NIFTY NOTION CALLED THE JEAN-A-MA-JIG (SEE SUPPLIES AND RESOURCES).

Shirt Options:
Short or long sleeves
Baseball jacket collar: Cut from ribbing, 4" wide by
2: 13½" long
4: 14" long
6: 14½" long
8: 15" long

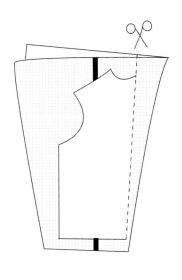

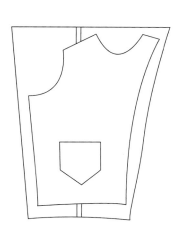

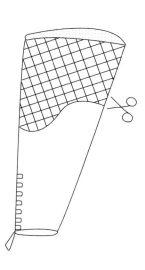

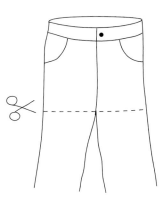

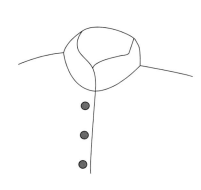

3 PRETTY CLOTHES

As I mentioned earlier in this book, pretty clothes do not need to be uncomfortable. In this chapter, I utilized the basic play clothing designs from the previous chapter, but added a few designer touches that won't interfere with kids on the go! By using different fabrics and fancy notions, your kids might not even notice. Sometimes they might surprise you and want to be just like grown-ups; that's when you throw in the tie like dad's!

HANDKERCHIEF SKIRT

You might find your little girl twirling and jumping when she's wearing this pointed shift. For some reason, the alternating points inspire just that. Paired with the eyelet blouse, you're guaranteed to have a well-dressed, comfortable girl!

Pattern Preparation: There are no pattern pieces for the skirt (see below), but you will need the Circle Template. Using the Circle Template, remove the waist opening.

3½"

Cutting: Cut 2 rectangles:
Size 2: 14", 7"

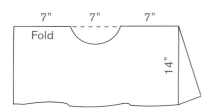

7"   7"   7"
Fold
14"

Finished skirt length 13½"
Size 4: 15", 8"

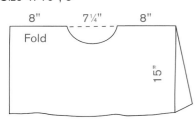

8"   7¼"   8"
Fold
15"

Finished skirt length 15½"
Size 6: 16", 9"

9"   7½"   9"
Fold
16"

Finished skirt length 17½"
Size 8: 18", 10"

10"   7¾"   10"
Fold
18"

Finished skirt length 20"
Cut 1 waistband 3" wide by
Size 2: 26" long
Size 4: 26½" long
Size 6: 27" long
Size 8: 27½" long

Materials and Notions

1 yard of 45" wide fabric
(size 8: 1¼ yards) fabric for
waistband
1" wide elastic to fit waist

DESIGNER SUGGESTION: FOR A PRO-
FESSIONAL LOOKING HEM, TRY USING
THE MITERED CORNER TECHNIQUE.
PRACTICE ON A SCRAP PIECE OF
FABRIC FIRST.

All seam allowances are 1/4" unless otherwise stated.

1. Hem the skirt by turning up 1/4" and then 1/4" again, or try using the mitered corner technique. Repeat on the second skirt (tier).

2. Place the two skirts together, alternating the direction of the rectangles.

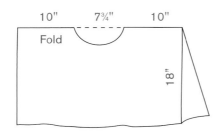

3. Press one long end of the waist-band toward the wrong side 1/4". With right sides together, close the short ends of the waistband to form a circle.

4. Sew the unpressed edge of the waistband to the waist, stretching waist if necessary. Stitch the inside of the waistband in place, leaving an opening to insert elastic.

5. Insert the elastic to fit the waist. Finish closing the opening.

Optional Decorative Pieces:
For a designer touch, you can appliqué hearts to the points and add pockets. You should do either before you put the two skirts (tiers) together.

1. Appliqué hearts (found on the pattern tissue) to the corners. Cut out and appliqué eight hearts to the skirt.

2. Pocket: Cut two 6" squares. With pocket pieces right sides together, sew all around, leaving an opening for turning. Clip the corners, turn, and press. Fold one corner down 2½". Topstitch around this small folded triangle and topstitch the pocket in place.

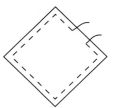

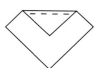

SHORT BLOUSE

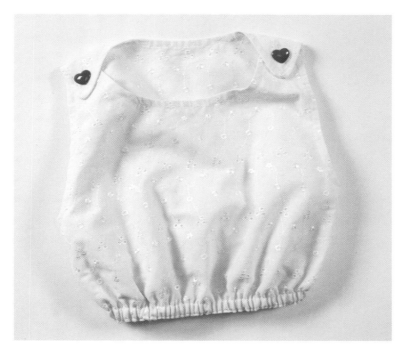

THE WHITE EYELET FABRIC GIVES THIS SHORT BLOUSE A EUROPEAN FLAVOR.
IT IS QUICK AND SIMPLE TO MAKE AND ALSO LOOKS GREAT WITH SHORTS.

Pattern Preparation: Use the Short Blouse pattern.

Cutting: Cut 2 fronts on fold (1 fabric, 1 lining). Cut 2 backs on fold (1 fabric, 1 lining). Follow the short blouse line.

Materials and Notions

1/2 yard of 45" wide fabric
1/2 yard lining fabric
2 buttons
Interfacing for button area
3/8" wide elastic for blouse bottom, length to fit waist (I used 24" on the medium)

All seam allowances are 1/4" unless otherwise stated.

1. Interface the fronts and backs at the shoulder tab areas for the button and buttonholes.

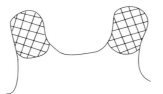

2. With right sides together, sew the front fabric and lining together around the armhole and neck. Repeat for the back. Clip the curves, turn, and press.

3. With right sides together, spread open the front and back side seams and sew the front to the back at the side seams, with right sides together. Press well.

4. Topstitch around the armholes and neck.

5. Elastic casing: Press the lower edge toward the wrong side 1/4" and then 1/2". Sew the casing in place, leaving an opening. Edgestitch close to the fold on the casing. Insert the elastic and close the opening.

6. Bring the back tab over the front. Make vertical buttonholes on the shoulder tabs and sew on the buttons.

HANDKERCHIEF DRESS

I USED RAYON FOR THIS SAMPLE, AND IT MAKES UP INTO A GREAT SUMMER DRESS. THE DRESS TOP IS THE SAME AS THE BLOUSE ON PAGE 59. THE BUTTONS AT THE SHOULDERS CREATE A FRESH LOOK. I USED THE SAME FABRIC FOR THE BLOUSE AND LINING.

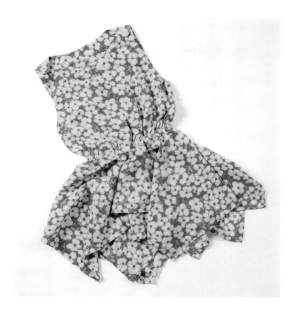

Pattern Preparation: Use the Short Blouse pattern. You will use the Circle Template for cutting the waist opening.

Cutting: Follow the exact measurements for the Handkerchief Skirt (page 57). Cut 2 skirts on fold. Follow the cutting lines for the dress on the bodice. Cut 2 fronts. Cut 2 backs on fold (1 fabric, 1 lining).

Materials and Notions

1¾ yards of 45" fabric
2 buttons
Interfacing for button area
3/8" wide elastic, length to fit waist (I used 23" of elastic on the small)

DESIGNER SUGGESTION: IF YOU HAVE TROUBLE FITTING THE BODICE INTO THE SKIRT, TRIM A VERY SMALL AMOUNT AWAY ON THE SKIRT'S WAIST OPENING.

All seam allowances are 1/4" unless otherwise stated.

1. Interface the fronts and backs at the shoulder tab areas for the button and buttonholes.

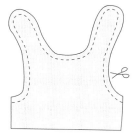

2. With right sides together, sew the two fronts (front and lining) together around the armhole and neck. Repeat for the back. Clip the curves, turn, and press.

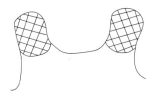

3. With right sides together, spread open the front and back side seams and sew the sides closed. Press well.

4. Topstitch around armholes and neck.

5. With right sides together, attach the bodice to the skirt. Do not attach the lining side, just the outer bodice, using a 3/8" seam. Trim seam allowance. Press up the raw edge of the bodice lining 3/8" toward the wrong side and edgestitch in place, leaving an opening to insert the elastic.

6. From the right side, stitch 1/2" from the first stitching. Insert the elastic just enough to gather the dress, but do not make it too tight.

7. Bring the back tab over the front. Make vertical buttonholes on the shoulder tabs and sew on the buttons.

HOODED SWEATER

This nautical looking outfit uses the Basic Sweatshirt pattern for the hooded top, and the skirt is constructed from simple rectangles. Of course, you could also make the top with short sleeves.

The sample shown was made out of a knit fabric, but you could try recycling an old sweater. If you use a sweater, avoid over-handling the cut-out pieces so they don't fray. Use woolly nylon in a serger and set the stitch width a little closer and make it a little wider.

Pattern Preparation: Follow the Basic Sweatshirt pattern, using the cutting on the placket line. Interface the front placket.

Cutting: Cut 2 fronts. Cut 1 back. Cut 2 sleeves, long or short. Cut 2 hoods.

Materials and Notions

1½ yards of 45" fabric
4 buttons
Interfacing
Optional: appliqué patch

All seam allowances are 1/4" unless otherwise stated.

1. With right sides together, sew the fronts to the back at the shoulders.

2. With right sides together, sew the sleeves in place to the arm openings.

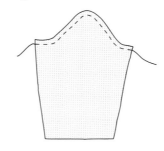

3. With right sides together, close the underarm and side seams.

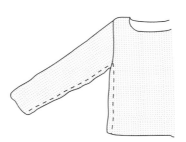

4. Press up the lower hem 1/2" and stitch in place.

5. With right sides together, sew the hood pieces together. Hem the front opening on the hood by turning its raw edge toward the inside 3/8" and down the straight side. Topstitch in place.

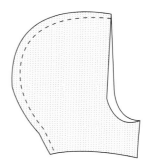

6. With right sides together, attach the hood to the shirt by matching the hood's center back to the shirt's center front. Wrap the placket around the hood toward the wrong side. Stitch the hood in place.

7. Turn the placket right side out and stitch in place.

8. Evenly space four buttonholes and sew on the buttons. Appliqué optional patch.

TIERED SKIRT

THIS SKIRT FEATURES TWO TIERS AND AN ELASTIC WAIST. IT IS EASY
TO SEW BECAUSE THE TIERS ARE JUST RECTANGLES!

Pattern Preparation: Note that there are no patterns for this project.

Cutting: Cut 2 tiers of each size on fold. Measurements are for height by length.

Size	2	4	6	8
Upper tier	6x7"	7x8"	8x9"	9x10"
Lower tier	10x13"	11x14"	12x15"	13x16"

Finished skirt length
Size 2: 12"
Size 4: 13"
Size 6: 14"
Size 8: 15"

Material and Notions

See the cutting chart at left for fabric requirements
1" wide elastic, length to fit waist
Optional: decorative elastic waistband

DESIGNER SUGGESTION: USE DECORATIVE ELASTIC FOR THE WAISTBAND.

All seam allowances are 1/4" unless otherwise stated.

1. With right sides together, sew the upper tier together on the short side to form a circle. Repeat for the lower tier.

2. Press up the hem on the lower tier 1/4" and then 1/4" again. Stitch the hem in place.

3. Gather the top edge of the lower tier to fit the bottom edge of the upper tier.

4. With right sides together and side seams matching, attach the upper tier to the lower tier.

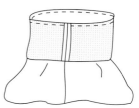

5. For the elastic casing, press the upper edge on the upper tier toward the wrong side 1/4" and then 1¼". Stitch in place, leaving an opening at center back. Insert the elastic and close the opening or attach decorative elastic waistband.

COUNTRY BIB JUMPER

THIS IS THE TIERED SKIRT (PAGE 65) WITH A BIB AND SUSPENDERS ADDED TO IT. PAIR IT WITH THE COUNTRY SHIRT FOR INSTANT COUNTRY FLAVOR.

Pattern Preparation: There are no pattern pieces for the skirt, but use the Bib pattern.

Cutting: Use the cutting chart from the tiered skirt (page 65). Cut 2 bibs and interface one side. Cut 2 straps (no pattern piece) 2-3/4" wide and (see Step 6)
Size 2: 14" long
Size 4: 16" long
Size 6: 18" long
Size 8: 20" long

Materials and Notions

See the cutting chart above for fabric requirements
Optional: rickrack
Optional: decorative buttons or latches for suspenders (these are strictly for looks and do not need to work)
1" elastic for waist and suspenders, approximately 2-1/2 yards
All seam allowances are 1/4" unless otherwise stated.

1. Sew the skirt the same as the Tiered Skirt (page 65), but press the edge down 1/4" and then 1¼" (instead of 1/4" twice).

2. Sew the casing in place, leaving an opening to insert the elastic at center front.

3. Sew the two bib pieces right sides together, leaving an opening at the top to turn and later insert the suspenders. Clip, turn, and press.

4. Fold straps in half lengthwise, right sides together, and sew the straps closed. Turn and press with the seam running down center back. Insert the elastic and secure at one end by sewing back and forth. Leave the elastic hanging out on the opposite end for now. (Your finished elastic length will be somewhere between 8" and 14". Do not cut the elastic yet.)

5. Position the bib with pins so the lower side points are even with the stitching from the casing. Insert the secured ends of the straps in the top of the bib. Insert the waist elastic, allowing it to stop and start where the bib is. Adjust the elastic to fit the waist and secure the ends while sewing the bib in place. Sew around the entire bib.

6. Finish the ends on the strap by determining the desired length. You may find it necessary to shorten the straps as well as the elastic. Turn the fabric's raw edge in 1/4" and secure the elastic ends. Stitch to the back of the skirt, following the stitching from the casing.

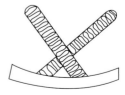

7. Embellish the skirt with rickrack and sew buckles or buttons to the front.

COUNTRY SHIRT

THE FRONT AND BACK PLEATS AND COVERED BUTTONS MAKE IT EASY TO MATCH THIS SHIRT WITH ANY OUT-FIT. IT CAN BE MADE WITH LONG (SHOWN) OR SHORT SLEEVES.

Pattern Preparation: Use the Basic Shirt pattern.

Cutting: Cut 2 fronts with the plackets interfaced. Cut 1 back on fold. Cut 2 collars (interfaced). Cut 2 cuffs (interfaced). Cut 2 sleeves. Cut 2 sleeve tabs 2" x 3" (no pattern piece). Interface the front placket and button area.

Materials and Notions

1⅓ yards of 45" wide fabric
6 5/8" buttons to cover with fabric
1/2 yard interfacing

All seam allowances are 1/4" unless otherwise stated.

1. Pin and press the pleats, as shown on the pattern, on the fronts and back toward the armholes and stitch in place.

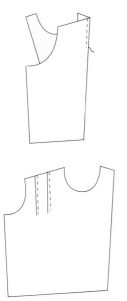

2. With right sides together, sew the fronts to the back at the shoulders.

3. With right sides together, sew the sleeve tabs in place by sewing up and down the line with a very small seam. Cut between the seam and turn the tab toward the wrong side and press. From the wrong side, turn the tab's raw edges under and stitch in place. You can make a point toward the top.

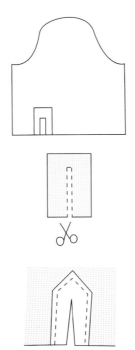

4. With right sides together, sew the sleeves in place to the arm openings.

5. Sew the sleeve and underarm seams closed. If you are making a short sleeve shirt, hem up the lower edge.

6. With right sides together, sew the short sides of the cuffs closed, forming circles. Matching raw edges, with right sides together, gather the lower edge of the sleeve to fit the cuff. Attach the cuff to the lower sleeve edge by sewing one half of the lower cuff edge to the sleeve. Turn to the inside and press the unsewn side 1/4". Stitch in the ditch. Repeat for other cuff and sleeve.

7. With right sides together, sew the collars together. Clip the curves and corners, turn, and press.

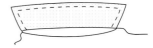

8. With right sides together and center backs matching, pin the collar in place. Wrap the placket around, catching the inside of the collar. The collar ends at the shirt's center front.

9. Turn the collar's remaining inside raw edge under 1/4" and stitch it to the shirt.

10. Turn and press the shirt and front placket. Press up the lower hem 1/4" and then 1". Stitch the hem in place and edgestitch the placket.

11. Cover the buttons with fabric. Evenly space four buttonholes down the front and one hole on each cuff. Sew the buttons in place.

DRESS PANTS

THESE PANTS ARE PERFECT FOR BOTH BOYS AND GIRLS. HERE, IT IS SHOWN WITH
THE COUNTRY SHIRT. DON'T FORGET TO MAKE THE MATCHING TIE!

Pattern Preparation: Use the Basic Pants pattern, following the built-in pocket on the front section.

Cutting: Cut 2 fronts (including built-in pocket). Cut 2 backs.

Materials and Notions

45" wide fabric:
Size 2: 1⅓ yards
Size 4: 1½ yards
Size 6: 1¾ yards
Size 8: 2 yards
1½ yards of 1" wide elastic

All seam allowances are 1/4" unless otherwise stated.

1. Press the pocket in place by folding it accordion-style, first to the back (wrong sides together) and then to the front on the foldlines marked on the pattern. The rounded bottom edges of the pocket should be even and the sides straight. Topstitch along the foldline that has the fabric wrong sides together first and then stitch the bottom of the pocket closed.

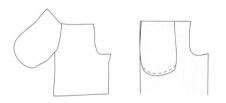

2. With right sides together, sew the fronts to the backs at the sides and inside leg seams.

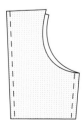

3. Turn one leg right side out and place it inside the leg that is inside out. Sew around the crotch in a horseshoe fashion. Turn right side out.

4. Press the top edge down 1/4" and then 1¼". Sew the casing in place, leaving an opening. Insert elastic to fit waist and close the opening.

5. Hem the pants by pressing up the lower raw edge 1/2" and stitch in place.

TIE

THIS IS JUST LIKE DADDY'S TIE, ONLY A SCALED-DOWN VERSION. IT'S THE PERFECT ACCESSORY TO THE COUNTRY SHIRT, GIVING THE WHOLE OUTFIT THAT SPECIAL-OCCASION LOOK.

Pattern Preparation: Use the Tie pattern pieces.

Cutting: Cut 1 of each tie piece from cotton. Trace the shaded area of the pattern and tape it together as one long piece. Cut 1 of polarfleece or Armorite for the tie interfacing.

Materials and Notions

1/2 yard of 45" wide cotton Polarfleece scrap or a piece of Armorite (You can take an old tie apart and use the fleece from inside of it.)

All seam allowances are 1/4" unless otherwise stated.

1. With right sides together, sew the two tie pieces together, making one long piece.

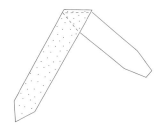

2. Place the facing down on the tie with right sides together and sew around the four sides. Clip the corners, turn, and press.

3. Place the fleece inside the tie, in the center, and press the tie around the fleece. Do not over-press.

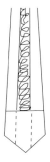

4. Close the back of the tie by handstitching.

4 PLAY TIME

The projects in this chapter just scream fun! Kids will be able to put on puppet plays, bike with the latest in helmet fashion, and go back to school in style.

COW BIKE HELMET

THIS IS A FUN AND INTRIGUING WAY TO COVER A BIKE HELMET. KIDS WILL BE MORE INSPIRED TO WEAR THE PROTECTIVE HEAD COVERING WITH A FUN, ALTERNATIVE COVER. THIS ONE IS FAST AND EASY TO MAKE AND SHOULD FIT ANY STANDARD-SIZE CHILD'S HELMET.

Pattern Preparation: Use the Helmet Cover and Horn patterns.

Cutting: Cut 4 horns. Cut 1 helmet cover.

Materials and Notions

2/3 yard cow print fabric
20" of 1/4" elastic
Black felt
Stuffing

1. Sew the four darts closed, using a 1/4" seam allowance, tapering the seam at the point. Trim the seam allowance back to 1/8" and zigzag the raw edge.

2. Press the hem toward the wrong side 1/8" and then 3/8". Stitch the casing in place, leaving an opening.

3. Insert the elastic and sew the opening closed. Check the fit on the helmet and make any necessary modifications to the darts.

4. Locate the position of the chin straps and make large button-holes, allowing the straps to come through.

5. Sew the horns using a 1/8" seam allowance, leaving an opening to turn and stuff. Stuff the horns well.

6. Position and baste the horns in place on the cover by hand.

7. Use a zigzag stitch to sew the horns in place.

DINOSAUR BIKE HELMET

HERE IS ANOTHER FUN WAY TO GET YOUR KIDS TO WEAR THEIR SAFETY HELMETS WHILE BIKING OR ROLLER BLADING. IT SHOULD FIT ANY STANDARD-SIZE CHILD'S HELMET.

Pattern Preparation: Use the Helmet Cover and Spikes patterns.

Cutting: Cut 1 helmet cover. Cut 2 spikes.

Materials and Notions

1/2 yard of fabric (helmet cover)
1/4 yard of fabric (spikes)
Stuffing
1/4" elastic

Note: Sew the spikes before cutting!

1. With the spike fabric right sides together, trace the spikes onto the fabric. Sew the tracing lines. Do not sew across the bottom.

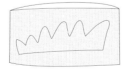

2. With right sides together, cut out the spikes, adding a 1/8" seam allowance. Clip in between the curves, turn, and press. Stuff the spikes and baste the bottom closed.

3. On the helmet cover, from center front to back, cut a 16" long slit down the middle. Sew the darts closed. Insert the spikes between the slit with the larger spikes facing toward the front or back. Sew the spikes in place.

4. Form a casing and finish the same as cow helmet (Steps 2 and 3).

STUFF SACKS

KIDS LOVE TO COLLECT ALL SORTS OF STUFF, LIKE MARBLES, SHELL, ROCKS, BASEBALL CARDS, AND BOTTLE CAPS. THESE SACKS ARE A GREAT WAY TO KEEP COLLECTIONS CONTAINED AND READY FOR VIEWING ANY TIME. YOUR FABRIC STASH IS PROBABLY LOADED WITH GREAT SCRAPS JUST FOR THIS PURPOSE, SO SEW A BUNCH! NOTE THAT NO PATTERN PIECES ARE NEEDED FOR ANY OF THESE SACKS.

DESIGNER SUGGESTION: FOR VERY SPECIAL COLLECTIONS, VELVET SACKS GO OVER WELL.

DESIGNER SUGGESTION: YOU CAN MAKE YOUR OWN DRAWSTRING TO COORDINATE WITH YOUR FABRIC (SEE SUPPLIES AND RESOURCES).

SQUARE-BOTTOM
DOUBLE-DRAWSTRING BAG

Pattern Preparation: Note that there are no patterns for this project.

Cutting: Cut a 7" x 18½" rectangle for the bag and two 7" x 5" strips for the drawstring casing.

Materials and Notions

See the cutting instructions above for fabric requirements
2 yards drawstring

All seam allowances are 1/4" unless otherwise stated.

1. With right sides together, sew the drawstring casing pieces to each end of the bag piece. Press the casing piece open. Press the raw edge of the casing 1/4" toward the wrong side.

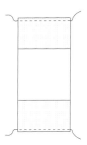

2. With right sides together, fold the bag piece in half crosswise and sew the side seams closed, starting from the bottom and toward the casing. Sew 1/4" into the casing and then backstitch. Lift the presser foot and move it up about 3/8". Continue sewing, backstitching at the start and finish. This will form the opening for the drawstring.

Press the casing in half, even with the seam where the casing is attached to the bag.

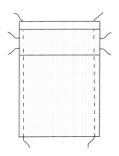

3. Pull the bottom of the bag open and sew across the bag's tips, about 1" in from the end.

4. From the wrong side, stitch the casing in place. Stitch a second time around the top edge. Turn bag right side out and press.

5. From one side, insert 1 yard of drawstring, entering and exiting through the same hole.

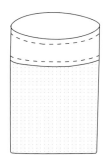

6. Repeat Step 5 from the opposite hole. Tie knots in the drawstring ends. To close the bag, pull on the drawstrings at the same time.

LINED, CIRCULAR-BOTTOM SINGLE-DRAWSTRING BAG

Pattern Preparation: Note that there are no patterns for this project.

Cutting: Cut 2 bottom circles, 4¼" in diameter (see page 88 for cutting a circle). Cut 2 bag pieces (1 is lining) 6½" x 12½". Cut 1 casing piece 5" x 12½".

Materials and Notions

See the cutting instructions above for fabric requirements
3/4 yard drawstring

All seam allowances are 1/4" unless otherwise stated.

1. With right sides together, sew the side seams on the bag piece. Repeat for lining.

2. With right sides together, sew the circular bottom to the bag piece. Repeat for lining. Turn both pieces right side out.

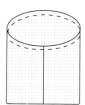

3. With right sides together, sew the short side of the casing. Sew 3/4", backstitching at the start and finish. Leave a 1/2" opening, sew the remaining casing, and backstitch. Press the casing seam open. Press the casing in half, right sides out. The drawstring opening should be on the outside.

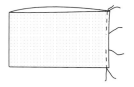

4. With right sides together, sew the casing to the outer bag piece with the opening closest to the bag. Turn inside out.

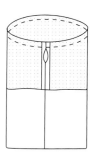

5. With the lining right side out, place it inside of the bag that is wrong side out. With raw edges even, sew around the top, leaving a 2" opening for turning.

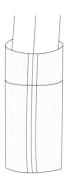

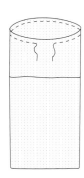

6. Turn everything right side out and press the bag with the casing pressed in half. Stitch around the bag close to the seam where the casing is attached to the bag. Topstitch around the upper edge.

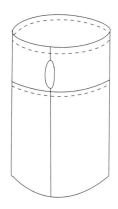

7. Insert the drawstring through the casing.

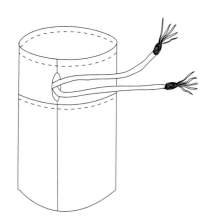

BASEBALL CARD POUCH

Pattern Preparation: Note that there are no patterns for this project.

Cutting: Cut 1 outer piece 13½" x 6".
Cut 1 lining 10¾" x 6".

Materials and Notions

See the cutting instructions
above for fabric requirements
1 snap
Scraps of interfacing

All seam allowances are 1/4" unless otherwise stated.

1. Fold the outer pouch piece in half lengthwise with right sides together. Sew across the short end.

2. Press the seam open to form a triangle. With the wrong side showing on the triangle, iron a scrap of interfacing to cover the top half of the triangle. Flip the piece over and repeat on other side. On this same side, interface the bottom edge with a 1" strip of interfacing.

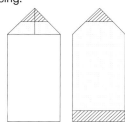

3. With right sides together, sew the lining to the pouch piece, across the short side where the triangle is.

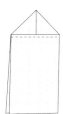

4. Sew down the sides, leaving an opening at the bottom for turning. Turn and press.

5. From the right side, topstitch across the bottom short end.

6. Fold the pouch to form an envelope shape. Topstitch around the entire pouch, closing the sides at the same time. Set snap on flap.

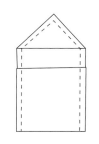

JEANS BACKPACK

NOW YOU CAN RECYCLE YOUR FAVORITE JEANS INTO A GREAT BACKPACK. IT IS SUPER QUICK TO STITCH UP.
THE BUILT-IN POCKETS ARE GREAT FOR SMALL EXTRAS, AND THE BELT LOOPS COME IN HANDY FOR THE DRAW-
STRING. OUR SAMPLE IS A SCHOOL-SIZE BACK PACK, BUT YOU CAN MAKE SMALLER PACKS USING SMALLER
JEANS (JUST MAKE YOUR FLAP PROPORTIONATE).

Pattern preparation: Use the Backpack Flap pattern.

Cutting: Cut 2 flap pieces; interface 1. Cut the jeans at the crotch where the legs start. Cut the legs open along the inside leg seam and use for the flap. The outside leg seam can run down the center of the flap.

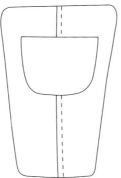

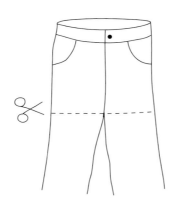

Materials and Notions

1 pair of medium-size adult jeans
2 quick-release clips for 1" wide webbing
2½ yards of 1" wide webbing
Interfacing for flap
1 snap
2 yards drawstring

All seam allowances are 1/4" unless otherwise stated.

1. From the webbing, cut two 6" pieces and slide the bottom half of the quick release clip on to each piece, folding the webbing in half. Position the clips on the back of the jeans, approximately 2½" to each side of the center rear seam. Baste in place through the back layer only.

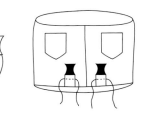

2. With right sides together, sew the bottom of the bag closed, backstitching where the clips are for extra strength.

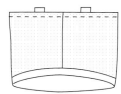

3. Pull the bottom of the bag apart and sew across the tips 1" in from the triangle's tip. Turn right side out.

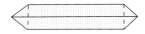

4. Insert the drawstring through the belt loops.

5. With right sides together, sew around the flap pieces, leaving an opening for turning at the top. Clip curves, turn, and press. Topstitch around the curved sides only, not the back. Press the flap's raw edges toward the wrong side.

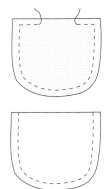

6. Position the flap to the bag, just above the drawstring. Cut the remaining webbing in half and insert the ends into the flap, 1" to each side of the center. Double-stitch the flap in place, catching the webbing.

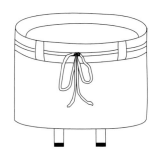

7. On the opposite ends, slide on the remaining half of the quick release clips. Adjust the webbing to fit. Set snap on flap.

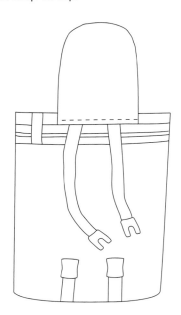

POP-UP PUPPET THEATER

This exciting puppet theater pops up and hangs from a single hook in an instant from a tree or clothesline. Your little ones will have a marvelous time conducting show after show. It is great for birthday parties or rainy day entertainment. The finished theater dimensions are 3 feet in diameter and 5 feet tall. The top is constructed from six sections and can be multicolored.

Pattern Preparation: Use the Pop-up Theater pattern.

Cutting: Cut 6 top sections and 25 scalloped trims. Cut the side wall and drapes as indicated below (no pattern pieces). Cut two tabs 2½" x 8" (no pattern pieces). Cut a 2½" x 12" strip for the hanging loop (no pattern piece).

Materials and Notions

Solid top: 2¼ yards fabric
Side wall: 82" x 44" fabric
2 drapes: 22" x 22" fabric
Piece under drapes 30" x 30" fabric
1/2 yard for scalloped trim (need total of 25 scallops)
6 snaps
20" of 1/4" elastic
2 16-gauge spring steel hoops, approximately 36" in diameter (see Supplies and Resources)

1/4" seam allowances are included.

1. **Circular top.** With right sides together, sew the top pieces together. Sew the seam from wide to narrow end, leaving any unevenness at the top (trim later). Press the seams to one side and from the right side topstitch each seam for extra reinforcement. Sew the last section to the first to complete the circular top.

2. **Finishing tent top.** With right sides together, fold the hanging loop in half lengthwise and sew the long side closed. Turn and press. Turn

the raw edge in at the top of the tent and pin the two ends of the strip (folded in half) in the center, forming a hook to hang the tent by.

3. **Scalloped trim.** Using the scallop pattern, make a total of twenty-five scallops. Piece the fabric together where necessary. Don't forget to add a 1/4" seam on the ends where piecing is necessary. With right sides together, baste to the circular top 3/4" in from the raw edge.

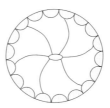

4. **Side walls.** Using the 82" x 44" piece, hem the two short sides and one long side by pressing 1/2" and then 1/2" again. Sew the unhemmed edge to the tent top, right sides together, 1/4" in following the basting. This will later form a casing where the spring hoops will go.

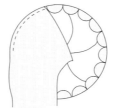

5. **Lower panel.** On the lower piece, form a casing across the top by pressing under 1/2" and then 1/2" again. Insert the elastic and secure at the ends. (The purpose of this elastic is to just take out the slack on the lower piece so it won't bag out.) Hem the other three sides and set this piece aside for now.

6. **Drapes.** On both drapes, hem the three sides only (sides and bottom). Attach to the top by filling in the opening and overlapping the drape pieces where they connect to sides and to each other. Sew all around the top, using a 3/4" seam allowance.

7. **Wires.** Insert the hoops in between the seam allowance of the top and the side walls (drapes) and pin in place. Using a zipper foot, sew the casing closed, using a 1/4" seam. Take care not to sew into the wires! You may find it easier to sew on the floor or on a big table where the whole hoop can rest flat on a surface.

8. **Drape tabs.** Sew the long sides of the tabs closed, turn, and press. Turn the raw ends in and stitch closed. Attach one end to the tent by using a snap on the opposite end. Attach a snap so you can wrap the tab around the drape and then snap it to hold it in place. Repeat for the other side.

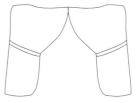

9. **Lower panel.** Matching the tent bottom, pin the lower panel in place under the drapes with the elastic at the top. Sew to one side of the tent. Use four snaps on the other side to allow it to open and close.

PUPPET THEATER CARRYING CASE

Materials and Notions

2 20" circles
2 2" x 32" gusset strips
22" nylon dress zipper
1 yard of 1" wide webbing

Pattern Preparation: Note that there are no patterns for this project.

Cutting: Using a thumbtack, string, and a pencil, make two circles on doubled fabric.

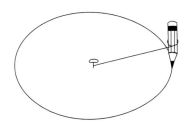

1. **Gusset.** Press one gusset piece in half lengthwise and find the center. Cut along the lengthwise crease 11" to each side of the center for the zipper. Cut at each end at an angle like an envelope.

2. **Zipper.** Baste and sew the zipper in place, turning the raw edges toward the wrong side. Piece the two gusset pieces together, using a 1/4" seam. Close the gusset to form a circle.

3. **Strap.** Sew the strap to each side of the zipper by sewing in a square and then an "X."

4. **Bag.** With right sides together, pin one circle to the gusset. If there is a direction to your print, watch that the zipper is at the top of your print. Sew the circle in place, using a 1/4" seam.

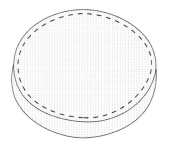

5. Open the zipper and pin the second circle in place. Sew in place, keeping the straps out of the way, using a 1/4" seam. Turn right side out through zipper opening.

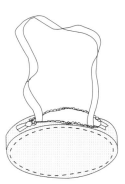

To put the theater away:

1. Twist the top once into a figure-eight.

2. Collapse the two circles in half.

3. The theater stows in its own compact carrying case.

DOLL OR STUFFED ANIMAL PLAY TENT

THIS CUTE TENT WORKS GREAT FOR BEAN BAG TOYS OR EVEN FASHION DOLLS. IT FOLDS FLAT AND THE POP-UP WIRES COME OUT FOR WASHING. THE FINISHED SIZE IS 14" x 14".

Pattern Preparation: Use the Tent pattern.

Cutting: Cut 2 tent bottoms 14¼" square (no pattern piece); interface 1. Cut 3 sides and 2 doors (1 can be lining); interface door. Cut 4 guides. Cut 2 36" x 1¼" strips for casing to cover taped wires (no pattern piece).

Materials and Notions

1½ yards of 45" wide fabric
1/2 yard of interfacing
14-1/4" square piece of fleece, denim, fur, etc. for tent bottom
2 33¼" pop-up spring steel wires (see Supplies and Resources)

Note: To prevent the sharp ends of the wires from poking through the fabric, wrap the ends securely with duct tape! This toy is not suitable for children under 3 years of age.

Serge or clean finish the raw edges.

1. **Front door.** With right sides together, stitch the front door panel to the lining at the opening. Clip the curves, turn, and press. Topstitch around the door opening. Baste all around the raw edges to keep the door and lining from slipping.

2. **Wire guides.** Fold the short ends of the guides 1/4" toward the wrong side and stitch in place. With wrong sides together, fold the guide in half lengthwise and press.

3. **Panels.** With right sides together, pin the two tent panels together. Place the wire guide on top, matching the raw edges and dots. Stitch the panels and guide in place. Repeat for the remaining panels, including the door.

4. Place the two tent bottoms together, right sides out. Baste the four edges together. Turn the tent inside out. Pin the right side of tent to the outer bottom side of the tent floor. Stitch in place. Turn the tent right side out.

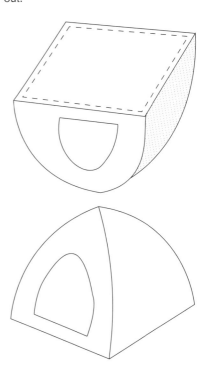

5. Fold the wire casing in half lengthwise, right sides together. Stitch and turn the casing. Insert the taped wire into the casing and tie knots at the ends.

6. Insert the covered wire into the tent from front to back in a diagonal fashion. Be sure to slip the covered wire through the wire guides attached at each seam.

SUPPLIES AND RESOURCES

Cordmaker
Clotilde, Inc.
1-800-772-2891
www.clotilde.com

Fold-over elastic
Birch Street Clothing, Inc.
1-800-736-0854
wwwbirchstreetclothing.com

Clotilde Inc.
1-800-772-2891
www.clotilde.com

Grommets
Snap Queen
1-800-736-0854

Jean-a-ma-jig
Clotilde Inc.
1-800-772-2891
www.clotilde.com

Kids prints
Zoo Dads
616-455-4570

Nylon Suplex
Available at most major fabric stores. Also known as flag fabric or jogging suit fabric, but should not be confused with rip stop nylon.

Seattle Fabrics
206-525-0670; fax 206-525-0779

Rain Shed Inc.
541-753-8900; fax 541-757-1887

Birch Street Clothing, Inc.
1-800-736-0854
wwwbirchstreetclothing.com

Quick release clips
Seattle Fabrics
206-525-0670; fax 206-525-0779

Ribbing
Seattle Fabrics
206-525-0670; fax 206-525-0779

Snaps
Clotilde Inc.
1-800-772-2891
www.clotilde.com

Nancy's Notions
1-800-833-0690
www.nancysnotions.com

Snap Queen
1-800-736-0854

Spring steel hoops and wires
Birch Street Clothing, Inc.
1-800-736-0854
www.birchstreetclothing.com

Stretch terry
Sewing Studio
1-800-688-9324

Mary's Stretch n Sew
619-589-8880

Stretch n Sew
1-800-547-7717
www-.-stret-ch-and-sew.com

PATTERN INDEX

QUICK AND EASY PROJECTS EVERYONE WILL LOVE

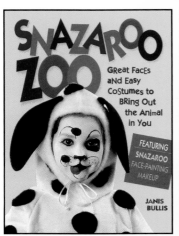

Snazaroo Zoo
Great Faces and Easy Costumes to Bring out the Animal in You
by Janis Bullis
Your kids will be wild about this dress-up zoo! One-piece patterns and face painting instructions for 18 different animal costumes are easy to follow and simple to make. Turn basic sweatsuits into frolicking fun with quick cutting and sewing. Includes instructions for accessories such as trunks, tails and antennas.

Softcover • 8-1/4 x 10-7/8
96 pages
color throughout
SZ • $12.95

More Polarfleece® Adventures
by Nancy Cornwell
Add designer touches to fleece with cutwork, sculpturing, appliqué, pintucking, fancy edge finishes, designer buttonholes, and machine embroidery. Start off with a quick refresher course and end with a chapter filled with fun fleece projects. In between, you'll find a new world of sewing loaded with templates and patterns for the designs featured.

Softcover • 8-1/4 x 10-7/8 • 160 pages
200 color photos • **AWPF2 • $19.95**

Bean Bag Toys
Easy-to-make Clothing, Furniture and Accessories
by Kathryn Severns
Includes are 16 adorable outfits, each with full-size patterns and simple, straight-forward instructions, so you can dress up your toys like a witch, cheerleader, barbecue chef, or pirate. In addition to clever outfits, furniture, and accessories, you are treated to party ideas from decorations, activities, and games to delicious recipes that will appeal to children of all ages.

Softcover • 8-1/4 x 10-7/8
112 pages
90 color photos
BBFF • $19.95

Sewing Tiny Toys
by Carolyn Vosburg Hall
Small plush toys are all the rage, and now you can quickly and easily create your own using such readily-available materials as felt, fake fur, beads, ribbons, pipe cleaners, and pellets. Included are patterns for 52 original animals like bears, dogs, and birds, complete with easy-to-follow instructions and clear illustrations. You will also learn how to create your own patterns from drawings or photos.

Softcover • 8-1/4 x 10-7/8 • 144 pages
200 illustrations • 75 color photos • **TOZ • $21.95**

Year Round Fun
by Bill Stephani
Everyone who works with kids will love this book filled with inexpensive projects for every occasion! Kids will find exciting projects to make and do from January through December with the quick and easy party ideas, group activities, Bible-school projects and much more. As an added bonus, the book contains an 8-page cutout section featuring the Delta Star X7 Shuttle Lander. It really flies!

Softcover • 8-1/4 x 10-7/8 • 96 pages
96 color photos
YRF • $14.95